HOW TO MAKE
SOFT CHEESES

Methods, recipes & tips for making

artisan soft cheeses at home.

Printed on FSC paper with Soy Ink

First Edition. ISBN: 978-0-9222647-5-8

CONTENTS

Ricotta Stuffed Zucchini Blossom

Mix Ricotta and fresh green herbs
with a little grated lemon zest. Put
teaspoonfuls in each blossom. Dip
in a medium batter and fry in hot oil
until they are golden. Serve with a
green summer salad.

FROM OUR KITCHEN

We are a small team at Country Trading Co.® and our recipes are tried in home kitchens, not labs. Our ingredients are real and so are we. In 2008 we packaged up what we knew and started selling our range of cheesemaking kits. We wrote these books to accompany our kits.

Over the years we have refined and added to our recipes, still testing them on family and friends and still making them in our home kitchens, just as you will.

Soft cheeses are a simple and wonderful introduction to artisan cheesemaking. All the photos in this book are of our own homemade cheeses. If some of them don't look perfect, it is because they aren't. Perfect food exists in factories, not kitchens! Enjoy.

Heather

Heather Cole - Home Cheesemaker & Chief Curd Stirrer

PS. Join us online to share your successes and questions. We love hearing from you.

GETTING STARTED

When we think of artisan cheeses our mind often goes to great cheeses such as Parmesan or Stilton. But the majority of the world's artisan cheese is soft, made often and eaten fresh.

Although many soft cheeses are factory produced nowadays, that is not how they originated. For centuries soft cheeses have been a means of turning small quantities of milk, sometimes from a variety of animals, into a nutritious source of protein.

These cheeses are artisan because of the historically close connection between milker and maker. They have always been homemade cheeses, made by hand, in small batches with fresh milk from available animals. Their recipes have evolved to suit climates, available flavorings and methods of preservation.

Few soft cheeses are recognized and protected by PDO or AOC regulations, but that does not lessen their merit. They are the most eaten cheeses in the world and that is always a good place to start.

As a home cheesemaker you will find more scope for experimentation and innovation in the world of soft cheese than any other family of cheeses. You can create your own artisan creation just as milkers and makers have done for generations before you.

THE SOFT CHEESE FAMILY

For a home cheesemaker it can be a bit confusing trying to work out the differences between soft cheeses. Let's face it, they're all gooey and white to varying degrees. So how do you tell your Fromage Blanc from your Crème Fraîche, or your Quark from your Sour Cream?

Each soft cheese has a traditional milk, method and means of storage that sets it apart from others. Soft cheeses are all subtly different and as you get to know them you'll learn which are good for what and how you like to make them.

We have grouped them into two families, the rich and creamy soft cheeses and the light and lean soft cheeses. We hope you'll make them all.

Cream Cheese

Crowdie

Fontainebleau

Paneer

Cottage Cheese

Herbed Ricotta

Labneh

Quark

Mascarpone

10

WHAT MILK TO USE?

Great cheese starts with great milk. Make sure it is fresh and has been stored at 38°F, 4°C. Even supermarket milk that is nearing its use by date can harbour unwanted bacteria. Soft cheeses are high in moisture, not pressed or aged and can be a breeding ground for unwanted bacteria such as *Listeria monocytogenes, Staphylococcus aureus* and other nasties. These bacteria can enter cheese from milk or from an unclean cheesemaking environment (see pg. 12).

People with a compromised immune system such as infants, the elderly and pregnant women can become seriously ill from eating cheese infected with these bacteria so every care should be taken when sourcing milk and making cheese.

Because soft cheeses don't age, their flavor comes largely from the milk they are made with. The better the milk, the better the flavor. Look for whole milk from organic, grass fed herds and avoid ultra heat treated and homogenized milks. The ingredients list should read simply milk.

We use fresh, pasteurized whole cow milk from the supermarket for our soft cheeses. If you are using sheep milk you will get a greater yield as it has a higher fat content. Goat milk is similar in fat content but easier to digest and has less lactose. Each soft cheese is best suited to a certain type of milk.

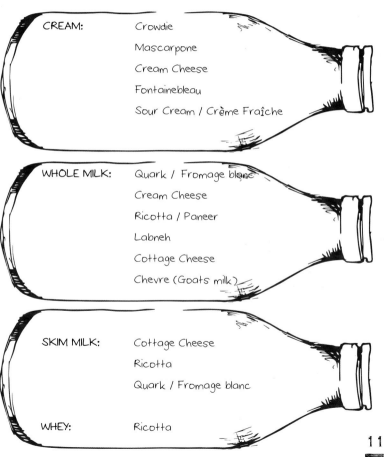

CREAM:
Crowdie
Mascarpone
Cream Cheese
Fontainebleau
Sour Cream / Crème Fraîche

WHOLE MILK:
Quark / Fromage blanc
Cream Cheese
Ricotta / Paneer
Labneh
Cottage Cheese
Chevre (Goats milk)

SKIM MILK:
Cottage Cheese
Ricotta
Quark / Fromage blanc

WHEY:
Ricotta

Keeping it Clean

When we look at the conditions and methods used to make soft cheeses throughout history we realize how sensitive to hygiene and food safety we have become in recent times. Bedouin tribes rolled small balls of soft cheese made from raw camel milk and then dried them in the sun of the desert to preserve them. Alpine German farmers would press soft Quark cheese into bricks and smoke it over a fire to preserve it. These practices would make the spines of food safety officials tingle today. Not that an awareness of food safety is a bad thing. We live in more modified environments than our ancestors did and our immune systems aren't as in-sync with local food sources as theirs were. Cleaning and sterilizing are key to making safe home dairy products. Do both. Don't skip either. Here are the methods that we use:

- Wash your hands thoroughly before making cheese. Sing Happy Birthday twice while you're doing it ensure you've washed and scrubbed for long enough! Hot soapy water, fingers to forearms, nails, palms and in-between fingers. Rinse and dry on paper towels.

- Before making cheese sterilize all equipment in a pot of boiling water and rinse any items that would be damaged by boiling water with very hot water.

- We prefer boiling water, but you can use household bleach in water to sterilize equipment. Follow instructions on the bottle carefully as too much bleach can kill culture and taint cheese.

- As soon as you finish making cheese, clean everything with a good scrub in very hot soapy water, rinse and then air dry equipment in a sunny spot before storing. A big clip top storage crate keeps gear clean and together between makes.

- When cleaning and sterilizing, let equipment drip dry rather than using the cloth in your kitchen which may be dirty.

- Sterilize a small plate with boiling water to sit your ladle, knife, and thermometer on during cheesemaking.

- Put a lid on cheese while culturing and draining to keep heat in and dust or insects out.

- Always start with fresh milk that is not near its use-by date. Raw milk can be pasteurized by heating to 161°F, 72°C for 1 minute and then immediately cooling to culturing temperature.

- If using raw milk, be very sure of its quality and the food safety program of the provider, keep it refrigerated and use on the same day of collection.

- Discard cheeses that smell or look different from usual

- Store soft cheeses in the refrigerator while draining and when completed, and label with both a creation and "eat-by" date.

Equipment

Making soft cheese does not require a big investment in specialized equipment. Most of the items you need will be found in your kitchen cupboards already, such as:

- Non-reactive saucepans, one inside the other to make a double boiler to stop milk burning while heating.

- Long thin knife for cutting curds.

- Non-reactive colander or sieve for draining cheese.

- Slotted spoon or ladle for stirring and scooping.

- Glass jars for storage.

We also use the following Country Trading Co.® products for making our soft cheeses:

- Dairy Thermometer - stainless steel with both °F and °C.

- Organic Cotton Cheesecloth - a fine weave for slow drainage and ease of cleaning is important.

- Soft Cheese Basket Molds - a range of shapes and sizes for making multiple cheeses or large singles.

- Fermenting Flask - an insulated flask can be useful to maintain temperature during longer incubations of some cultured soft cheeses, especially during winter when room temperatures may be lower. Electric yogurt makers run at too higher temperature for making soft cheeses, but a good flask will hold the temperature of the milk you put into it for at least 10-12 hours.

MAKING CURDS

Little Miss Muffett sat on her tuffet eating her curds and whey is the nursery rhyme from childhood and these curds are the starting point for all simple soft cheeses. The act of turning milk into solid curds and liquid whey is known as coagulating or setting the milk.

You can make curds for soft cheeses in three main ways:

1. Add an animal or vegetable based rennet enzyme that binds the casein molecules in the milk together to make a wobbly solid.

2. Acidify the milk with lemon juice or vinegar which quickly curdles the milk into lumpy solids.

3. Acidify the milk with lactic starter culture over a longer period and as the starter converts the lactose (sugars) into lactic acid the milk will form a soft curd.

All of these methods lead to the milk solids binding together into curds that can then be scooped off and worked by the cheesemaker into a variety of soft cheeses.

There are many different rennets available with varying strengths and properties. Our recipes use vegetarian rennet from the Culture Cupboard®. If you are using another rennet, follow the instructions on the product. It is important to use the correct quantity of rennet for the type of cheese you are making and quantity of milk you are working with.

CULTURED OR UNCULTURED?

Soft cheeses can be cultured or uncultured. Uncultured cheeses are made by acidifying or rennetting milk and are often referred to as "fresh cheeses".

Cultured cheeses are made with the addition of lactic bacteria starter cultures which take the milk one step closer to "proper" cheese in flavor and texture.

Our cultured soft cheese recipes use starter cultures from the Culture Cupboard®. If you use other brands of culture, choose a mesophilic starter that contains *Leuconostoc mesenteroides ssp. cremoris and the following Lactococcus sub-species - lactis, cremoris and lactis biovar. diacetylactis*. These will help create the flavors and aromas in your soft cheeses.

CULTURED	UNCULTURED
Quark	Crowdie
Cottage Cheese	Mascarpone
Labneh	Paneer
Cream Cheese	Ricotta
Sour Cream	
Crème Fraîche	
Lactic Curd Cheese	

SALT & ADDITIVES

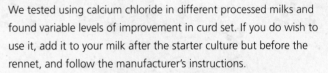

We take a hands off approach to additives. They are often used to overcome poor quality ingredients and either speed up or slow down Mother Nature. If it doesn't contribute to the quality or safety of the cheese, we think you can do without it.

You will often see calcium chloride used in home cheesemaking recipes to replace calcium lost in milk processing and storage. It is a natural mineral salt that is used to improve curd strength and increase yield. We don't include it in our recipes or kits because we believe that if you are using fresh, good quality milk it is an unnecessary additive.

We tested using calcium chloride in different processed milks and found variable levels of improvement in curd set. If you do wish to use it, add it to your milk after the starter culture but before the rennet, and follow the manufacturer's instructions.

Salt is an important and natural additive in the cheesemaking process. It draws whey from the curds to help dry the cheese. It preserves, adds flavor and plays an important part in the bacterial dance taking place in a cultured cheese. Don't try to omit salt from the recipes.

Salt is like sugar; you can get refined white and you can get raw and unprocessed. Table salt is the most processed and can contain added iodine and anti-caking agent chemicals. Iodine is a sterilizing agent that can kill or inhibit cheese cultures.

Anti-caking agents are not as damaging to the cheese, but are not necessary for the cheesemaking process. Kosher salt and most brands of flaked sea salt or rock salt are free from iodine but may contain anti-caking agents, so read the label. Brining and pickling salt is usually free from both additives.

We use Country Trading Co.® Natural Sea Salt, which is evaporated from New Zealand ocean waters, free from both iodine and anti-caking agents.

FLAVORING SOFT CHEESES

Soft cheeses can be easily flavored with combinations of spices, herbs and other natural seasonings. They give the cheesemaker a lot more freedom to innovate with flavorings than hard cheeses. Because soft cheeses are kept under refrigeration and used quickly, flavorings can be fresh. Here are some of our favorites.

Lemon Thyme Labneh

Sweet Chili Pepper Cream Cheese

Paprika Quark

Cottage Cheese & Chives

Chocolate Mascarpone

Honey Ricotta Drizzle

STORING SOFT CHEESES

Soft cheeses are typically high in moisture and low in salt, so they are not aged for long periods like hard cheeses. When making soft cheese at home we recommend making small batches and eating within a few days of making.

Store your soft cheeses in a sealed jar or container in the refrigerator. Some soft cheeses also freeze well. Because a lot of soft cheeses are used in cooking, having some frozen portions to hand can be really useful. Defrost them slowly in the refrigerator for best results.

Traditionally, soft cheeses were pressed and smoked, sun-dried and coated in waxes or stored in brine or oil to preserve them further. Nowadays these methods are used more for enhancing flavor and presentation than preserving the cheese.

Try these traditional storage methods to turn your simple soft cheeses into exquisite artisan gifts. Just be sure to label with an "eat by" date and instruct the recipient not to store it with the camels like the Bedouins did. The refrigerator is still the safest place for your soft cheese, even if it is salted, smoked or packed in oil.

SALTING

Salt transforms soft cheeses, enhancing the flavor and keeping qualities. Ricotta Salata is firm slicing cheese made by salt rubbing and drying a fresh Ricotta cheese over several days (see pg. 38).

STORING IN OIL

Mix Labneh with fresh chopped herbs and roll into small balls. Store in a jar with a good fruity olive oil and some strips of lemon peel. The oil stops the balls sticking together. We don't recommend oil storage for extending the shelf-life of soft cheeses and we do recommend refrigeration for oil stored cheeses.

SMOKING

Acid coagulated cheeses such as Paneer and Ricotta can be hot smoked without melting. This is the quickest way to turn a simple soft cheese into an artisan cheese board centerpiece (see pg. 39).

FREEZING

We've found higher fat soft cheeses such as Mascarpone, Cream Cheese and Sour Cream can freeze quite well for a month or two. Thaw slowly in the refrigerator for best results. They are not as good as fresh cheeses - you will get some separation, but stirring will recombine and they're fine for use in cooking.

DREAMY CREAMY SOFTIES

These creamy soft cheeses are somewhere between a butter and a cheese. Don't be concerned about their fat content as they are so high in moisture that their fat content per ounce is very similar to other cheeses.

Knowing how to make creamy cheeses at home not only saves you money, but equips you with an indispensable range of ingredients for rich desserts, creamy sauces, cheesecakes and baked goods.

MASCARPONE

Mascarpone cheese is closer to a butter than a cheese. It is cream that has been acidified with lemon juice or citric acid to remove whey and turn it thick and creamy. Perfect for rich desserts like Tiramisu, and Torta di Mascarpone - a layered cheesecake with your choice of fillings such as salmon and cucumber or blue cheese, basil, pine nuts and Parmesan.

Time: 1 hour to make, 5-8 hours to drain. Yield: 11 ½ oz (330 g) Mascarpone.

2 cups (450 ml) Cream (approx. 36% fat)
3 tablespoons Lemon juice

Non-reactive saucepans to make a double boiler
Non-reactive sieve
Country Trading Co.® Dairy Thermometer
Country Trading Co.® Organic Cotton Cheesecloth
Glass storage jar with lid

1. Sterilize all equipment - refer page 12.

2. Gently heat the cream in a double boiler until it reaches 185°F, 85°C.

3. Remove from the heat and slowly stir in 2 tablespoons of lemon juice with a large spoon. The cream should start to thicken slightly and coat the back of the spoon.

4. Stir in the remaining lemon juice and set aside to cool for 30 minutes.

5. Line a sieve with a double layer of cheesecloth and place it over a bowl.

6. Scoop the Mascarpone into the lined sieve. For a soft Mascarpone drain it in the refrigerator for 4-5 hours. For a firmer cheese let it drain overnight. If you find it is too firm you can whisk in a little of the drained whey until it reaches the desired consistency.

7. Transfer to a glass jar with a lid and use within 2–3 days. Sweeten with confectioner's sugar for use in desserts.

CREAM CHEESE

The original cream cheese is a very old French cheese known as Neufchâtel but today most of us think of cream cheese as a sweet and slightly salty solid block, wrapped in foil. This variety of cream cheese was first made in America in the late 1800s and is still a vastly popular processed cheese today. Lots of testing went in to our homemade version of cream cheese with no stabilizers added!

Time: 1 ½ hours to make, 23 hours to culture and press. Yield: 12 oz (350 g) cream cheese.

10 oz (300 ml) Whole cream (approx. 35% fat)
24 oz (700 ml) Homogenized whole milk
1 Culture Cupboard® Soft Cheese sachet
½ Culture Cupboard® Rennet sachet
¼ cup Non-chlorinated water*
¼ teaspoon Natural sea salt (additive free)

Non-reactive pans to make a double boiler
Non-reactive colander
Country Trading Co.® Dairy Thermometer
Country Trading Co.® Organic Cotton Cheesecloth
Country Trading Co.® Fermenting Flask or
1 quart (1 liter) wide mouth vacuum food flask
Country Trading Co.® Large Square Soft Cheese Basket or
1 quart (1 liter) soft cheese basket

* Boiling water for 15 minutes will remove chlorine present. Let water cool completely before adding rennet.

1. Sterilize all equipment - refer page 12.

2. Gently heat the milk and cream in a double boiler until it reaches 194°F, 90°C. This improves the thickness of the finished product.

3. Cool the milk mixture to 68°F, 20°C by placing the pan in a sink of cold water for 15-20 minutes.

4. When the temperature is reached, remove the pan from the water, add the Soft Cheese culture from the sachet and stir until well mixed. Culture for 1 hour.

5. Warm the soft cheese maker or vacuum flask by filling it with boiling water for a couple of minutes. Check the temperature of the cultured milk mixture and reheat to 68°F, 20°C before pouring it into the container and putting it in the maker or flask.

6. Mix the rennet with the cool, non-chlorinated water and gently stir through the milk until well mixed.

7. Put the lid on the maker or flask and leave to culture for 12-18 hours, or until the curd has set into a solid mass.

8. Open the maker or flask, cut the curd into 1 inch (2.5 cm) cubes and let it rest for 5 minutes.

9. Line a non-reactive colander or sieve with a double layer of sterilized cotton cheesecloth and place over a bowl to catch the whey. Ladle the curds into the colander and drain in the refrigerator for 4 hours.

10. Transfer the drained curds to a large mixing bowl and sprinkle with the salt. Whisk the curds and salt together with a large whisk until smooth and well combined.

11. Line the basket mold with sterilized cheesecloth and fill with the salted curds, folding the cheesecloth over the top to seal.

12. Place the mold on a draining tray and put it in the refrigerator to drain for a further 10 hours.

13. Unpack the drained cream cheese and store in a covered glass container in the refrigerator. Use within 14 days.

Cream Cheese Tips

* Maintain the correct temperature during culturing.

* Use homogenized milk - it is the only cheese we recommend this for!

* Don't use extra cream - you will actually get a creamier result if the finished fat content is around 10-12%.

CRÈME FRAÎCHE (SOUR CREAM)

Crème Fraîche, or sour cream, is a natural cultured cream, free from the artificial thickeners and stabilizers found in many store bought sour creams. Use it to thicken sauces and as a topping for baked potatoes. It will be slightly thinner than commercial sour cream and can be strained through cotton cheesecloth to create a thicker cream if desired.

Time: 30 minutes to make, 36 hours to culture, cool and set. Yield: 1 lb (450 g) Crème Fraîche.

1 pint (500 ml) Whole cream (approx. 35% fat)
½ Culture Cupboard® Soft Cheese sachet

Non-reactive pans to make a double boiler
Non-reactive colander
Country Trading Co.® Dairy Thermometer
Country Trading Co.® Fermenting Flask or
Wide-mouth vacuum food flask

1. Sterilize all equipment - refer page 12.

2. Gently heat the cream in a double boiler until it reaches 194°F, 90°C. This improves the thickness of the finished product.

3. Cool to 77°F, 25°C by placing the pan in a sink of cold water for about 5 minutes.

4. Remove pan from the water, add the culture from the sachet and mix well.

5. Warm the flask and container with hot water. Pour the cultured milk into the container and put it in the flask to culture.

6. Put the lid on the maker or flask and leave to culture for 12 hours, or until the curd has set into a solid mass.

7. Allow to cool completely, pack into sterilized glass jars with lids and refrigerate for a further 12 hours before use.

8. Label, date and use within 1 week.

CROWDIE

This ancient Scottish cheese dates from Viking times. It has enjoyed a recent revival by artisan Scottish cheesemakers who claim it is a good food to have before a ceilidh (party) to counteract the affects of whisky! It is a very mild, uncultured, curd cheese that is then whipped together with cream and sometimes coated in oatmeal and peppercorns.

Time: 30 minutes to make, 9 hours to set and drain. Yield: 1 lb (450 g) Crowdie.

....

1 quart (1 liter) Whole milk
½ Culture Cupboard® Vegetarian Rennet sachet
¼ cup Non-chlorinated water*
3 oz (90 ml) Whole cream (approx. 35% fat)
½ teaspoon Natural sea salt (additive free)

Non-reactive pan
Slotted spoon
Non-reactive colander
Country Trading Co.® Dairy Thermometer
Country Trading Co.® Organic Cotton Cheesecloth

1. Sterilize all equipment - refer page 12.

2. Heat the milk in a medium sized non-reactive pan to 89°F, 32°C and remove from the heat.

3. Mix the rennet in the water and pour gently into the warmed milk over the back of a slotted spoon. Stir to combine.

4. Put a lid on the pan of milk and sit it somewhere warm for 3 hours, or until well set.

5. Line a non-reactive colander with sterilized cotton cheesecloth and place over a bowl.

6. Cut the set curds into a checkerboard pattern of 1 inch (2.5 cm) cubes and pour into the colander.

Boiling water for 15 minutes will remove chlorine present. Let water cool completely before adding rennet.

7. Leave to drain for 6 hours in the refrigerator then scoop the curds into a clean mixing bowl and mix in the cream and salt with a whisk.

8. Store in a covered glass jar in the refrigerator and use within 7 days.

Crowdie Tips

Wet your hands and roll the drained cheese into a log or little balls, coat with pinhead oatmeal and ground black peppercorns.

Refrigerate to firm up. Try adding fresh herbs & spices for a savory creamy spread.

FONTAINEBLEAU

This rich, fresh, French cheese is made by combining Fromage Blanc with whipped cream. Fontainebleau is a delicate, foamy, dessert cheese that is best made and consumed on the same day. It is perfect with fresh berries or syrups. Make well drained Fromage Blanc a full day before you want to make Fontainebleau. The recipe can easily be scaled up to serve a crowd.

Time: 15 minutes to assemble with ready-made Fromage Blanc. Yield: 1 lb (500 g), serves 4.

1 cup Whole cream (approx. 35% fat)
9 oz (250 g) Fromage Blanc (pg. 42)
Fresh berries
Honey

1. Whip the cream until stiff.

2. In a separate bowl whisk the Fromage Blanc until well blended and smooth.

3. Reserve ½ a cup of whipped cream for topping.

4. Fold the remaining whipped cream through the Fromage Blanc gently with a metal spoon until loosely combined.

5. Fill four small pots with Fontainebleau and top with reserved whipped cream.

6. Decorate each pot with fresh berries and a good drizzle of honey before serving.

Fontainebleau Tips

It is traditionally sold and served in small cheesecloth-lined pots to keep the whipped texture intact.

The magic is in the lightness of the cheese so make it just before serving. If it sits around it goes flat.

Add a little natural vanilla or cinnamon to the whipped cream for sweetness.

Try topping it with sweet berry puree and flaked almonds.

Light and fluffy pillows of Fontainebleau

FRESH & LEAN SOFTIES

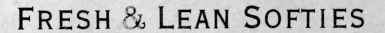

Not all soft cheeses are rich and creamy. Many are made from whole milk or skimmed milk and are great for everyday eating. They are an excellent source of protein, vitamins and minerals. We guarantee when you make these cheeses in your own kitchen with tangy culture and quality milk, they will not suffer the label of bland and boring "low fat" food.

TRADITIONAL COTTAGE CHEESE

Known to dieters the world over as a low calorie, high protein cheese, commercial cottage cheese is quite bland in flavor compared to traditional slow-cultured cottage cheese. Once you taste this traditional cottage cheese you will want to make and eat it whether you are watching your calories or not!

Time: 1 ¼ hours to make, 12 hours to culture. Yield: 1 lb (450 g) cottage cheese.

....

2 quarts (2 liters) Whole milk or skimmed milk
1 Culture Cupboard® Soft Cheese sachet
2 quarts (2 liters) Chilled water with a squeeze of lemon juice in it
½ teaspoon Natural sea salt (additive free)
1 tablespoon Cream (optional)

Non reactive pan, colander, knife and slotted spoon
Country Trading Co.® Dairy Thermometer
Country Trading Co.® Organic Cotton Cheesecloth

1. Sterilize all equipment - see page 12.

2. Heat the milk in a non-reactive pan to 77°F, 25°C.

3. Remove from heat, add the culture sachet and mix well.

4. Leave the milk in the pan to culture for 12 hours at 77°F, 25°C, or until the curd has set into a solid mass. If you are in a cool room, placing the pan in a water bath will help keep the temperature constant during culturing, replacing water with more hot as required to maintain milk temperature.

5. When set, slice the curd into 1 inch (2.5 cm) squares. Let it rest for 5 minutes.

6. Heat the curds slowly over 50 minutes, stirring occasionally with a slotted spoon until the heat reaches 129°F, 54°C. The curds will gradually form into small balls.

7. Place a colander lined with sterilized cotton cheesecloth over a sink and slowly pour the curds in to drain.

8. Gently pour the chilled water and lemon juice over the curds to rinse and set them.

9. Drain well and gently mix through salt and optional cream.

10. Pack in glass jars, store in the refrigerator and eat within 7 days.

FAST COTTAGE CHEESE

This cottage cheese is easier and faster to make and relies on the addition of yogurt to provide the depth of flavor of traditional cottage cheese made without rennet. If you are in a hurry and plan to add herbs or flavorings to the finished cheese, then that may not be such a concern.

Time: 45 minutes to make 1½ hours to culture. Yield: 1 lb (500 g) cottage cheese.

....

2 quarts (2 liters) of Whole milk or skimmed milk
1 Culture Cupboard® Soft Cheese sachet
3 tablespoons Natural unsweetened yogurt
1 Culture Cupboard® Vegetarian Rennet sachet
¼ cup Non-chlorinated water*
2 quarts (2 liters) Chilled water with a squeeze of lemon juice
½ teaspoon Natural sea salt (additive free)
1 tablespoon Cream (optional)

Non-reactive pan, colander, slotted spoon
Country Trading Co.® Dairy Thermometer
Country Trading Co.® Organic Cotton Cheesecloth

*Boiling water for 15 minutes will remove chlorine present. Let water cool completely before adding rennet.

1. Sterilize all equipment with boiling water and shake off excess water.

2. Heat the milk in a non-reactive pan to 89°F, 32°C.

3. Remove pan from the heat, add the soft cheese culture, yogurt, mix well and set aside to culture for 30 minutes.

4. Mix the rennet into the non-chlorinated water and pour gently into the warmed milk over the back of a slotted spoon. Gently stir to combine.

5. Put the pan aside with the lid on in a warm place to set for 60 minutes, or until the curd breaks cleanly when cut with a knife.

6. Slice the curd into 1 inch (2.5 cm) cubes. Let it rest for 5 minutes then heat gently over 30 minutes, stirring occasionally with a slotted spoon until the heat reaches 126°F, 52°C. The curds will form into small balls.

7. Line a colander with sterilized cotton cheesecloth and slowly pour the curds into the colander.

8. Gently pour the chilled water and lemon juice over the curds to rinse and set them.

9. Drain well, mix through salt and optional cream. Pack in glass jars, store in the refrigerator and eat within 7 days.

Cottage Cheese Tips

Don't heat too fast or the curds form a thick skin and whey gets trapped inside making flabby curds. Slow heating makes nice springy, squeaky curds.

The lemon juice slightly acidifies the water and helps stop the cheese going slimy during storage.

LACTIC CURD CHEESES

This family includes a large number of fresh and aged soft cheeses, made from a range of milks. They are traditionally cultured for longer periods at lower temperatures with little or no added rennet. Our instruction to make a lactic cheese is something that you follow once you have mastered the basics and can adapt a method to your needs rather than follow a recipe.

Time: As long as it takes. Yield: As much as you make.

Sterilize your equipment and heat your milk to 77°F, 25°C. Add a mesophilic starter such as the Culture Cupboard® Soft Cheese Starter and stir to dissolve. Still the milk and add a small amount of rennet - half the manufacturers dose for the amount of milk you are culturing is usually sufficient.

The soft curds of a lactic cheese are formed mainly by the acidification of the milk over a long time frame, but a little rennet can help to form firmer curds.

Cover the pot and place it somewhere where the temperature will not fall below 68°F, 20°C while it cultures. Check it after 8 hours. When the curd has formed a solid wobbly block and you see some clear liquid whey covering it then it is ready to cut and drain. If it hasn't formed a solid block leave it at the same temperature for up to 24 hours but check it regularly as you don't want to over-culture or it produces a dry grainy curd with a bitter taste rather than a fresh sweet curd.

Line a colander with sterilized cotton cheesecloth and place it over a large bowl to catch the whey. Carefully ladle in the set curds, cover with cheesecloth and leave them in a draught free place at the same 77°F, 25°C temperature to drain for 12-16 hours. Once the curds have drained put them in a clean bowl and mix through salt to taste. We like to weigh the curds and add 2% of the weight of the curds in salt. The curds can then be stored in the refrigerator, shaped by hand, topped with herbs and eaten within a week.

For aging these lactic curd cheeses you can also ladle them into a range of hoops and molds to drain and then surface rub them with salt to the same percentage. Mature them in the refrigerator in a cheese box with a mat and turn them frequently. Eat within 2-3 weeks. These aged lactic cheeses often have the addition of molds or ash to enhance the surface. See our Camembert & Brie book for more information.

MILK RICOTTA / QUESO BLANCO

Ricotta is a low fat cheese, traditionally made by extracting the remaining protein from whey. Fresh whey leftover from another batch of cheese such as Mozzarella is ideal but you need a lot. This whole cow milk Ricotta produces a greater yield and creamier cheese than traditional whey Ricotta. It is almost identical in method to the popular Latin American fresh cheese Queso Blanco.

Time: 60 minutes to make, 4 hours to drain. Yield: 12 oz (340 g) Ricotta.

2 quarts (2 liters) Whole cow milk
1 teaspoon Natural sea salt (additive free)
3-4 tablespoons White vinegar

Large non-reactive pans to make a double boiler
Slotted spoon
Country Trading Co.® Dairy Thermometer
Non-reactive colander and
Country Trading Co.® Organic Cotton Cheesecloth, or
Country Trading Co.® Large Round Soft Cheese Basket

1. Sterilize all equipment - see page 12.

2. Pour the milk into a double boiler and heat to 190°F, 88°C.

3. Gently stir in the salt and continue heating to 195°F, 90°C then remove from the heat.

4. Pour 3 tablespoons of vinegar into the pan of milk over the back of a slotted spoon, then stir gently and briefly and leave to sit for 15 minutes while the curd forms.

5. Take a slotted spoon and gently move the curds into the center of the pot. You should have soft, pillowy, white curds and clear, straw yellow whey if you have a good yield. If the curd hasn't formed add another tablespoon of vinegar and leave for 5 minutes.

6. Ladle the curds gently into a basket mold or cheesecloth lined colander and let them drain uncovered in the refrigerator for at least 4 hours. The longer you drain them the firmer the cheese will be.

7. Gently remove from the basket and store in a covered container in the refrigerator. Eat within 3-4 days.

CHILI RICOTTA SALATA

Ricotta Salata is a dried, seasoned Ricotta from southern Italy. Fresh Ricotta is made as usual, but the chili flakes, salt and additional draining and salting time creates a harder cheese that can be used for grating and slicing.

Time: 10 days to make. Yield: 9 oz (260 g) Ricotta Salata.

1 batch of Milk Ricotta (pg. 36), ready to mold
1 teaspoon Chili flakes
2 teaspoons Natural sea salt (additive free)

1. Prepare a batch of Milk Ricotta and when it is ready to mold, mix through the chili flakes and 1 teaspoon of salt.

2. Ladle the curds and chili flakes into the mold to drain.

3. Allow the Ricotta to drain for 12 hours, covered in the refrigerator, then un-mold and turn the cheese, returning it to the mold.

4. Find a container that will go inside the mold that can balance a weight on top. Place approx. 1 lb (450 g) of weight on the cheese. Press for 24 hours, turn the cheese and press for a further 24 hours.

5. Remove the cheese from the mold, rub with ½ a teaspoon of salt and sit on a draining tray in a sealed container stored in the refrigerator.

6. Over the course of a week, rub a further ½ teaspoon of salt into the cheese. Turn it daily, change the sushi mat and wipe any moisture from the container.

7. Store the cheese in the refrigerator in a sealed container for up to a further month, turning occasionally and eat within 7 days once cut.

SMOKED RICOTTA

Ricotta Affumicata della Mammola is a smoked Ricotta traditionally made from goat milk, laid on a bed of chestnut leaves, wrapped in ferns and then gently smoked over a wood fire fed with fragrant herbs. The resulting cheese takes on a smoky coloring, a firmer texture and earthy smoked herb flavor. Cow milk Ricotta makes a good substitute for this recipe.

Smoking Time: 3-5 hours.

1. Prepare a batch of Milk Ricotta (pg. 36) and allow to drain for at least 12 hours.

2. Rub the cheese with 1 teaspoon of natural sea salt and dry it for a further 24 hours in a cool place.

3. Smoke the cheese in a hot smoker for 3-5 hours on a bed of herbs such as rosemary, using a fragrant wood like apple, maple or hickory. Ricotta doesn't melt like rennet coagulated cheese, so a hot smoker can be used for quick results and to aid forming a dry rind.

4. Cool and dry the cheese for a further 2-3 hours at room temperature.

5. Store in the refrigerator in a sealed container for up to a further 2 weeks and eat within 3-4 days once cut.

Sea Water Rikotta

The legendary Ricotta pops up in many different countries under many different names. Here is a particularly fun one from the island of Malta, south of Sicily. As a coastal community, it makes sense to use what resources are to hand and fresh salty sea water is the perfect ingredient to set the Ricotta curds floating. Try it next time you are at an unpolluted beach.

Time: 3-5 hours. Yield: 9 oz (250 g) Rikotta

....

2 quarts (2 liters) Whole cow milk
2 quarts (2 liters) Pristine sea water

Non-reactive pan, colander and cheesecloth

1. Heat the milk to just below boiling. You probably won't have a thermometer with you but when bubbles start to appear and steam is rising it will be hot enough.

2. Add the sea water to the milk, gently stir through and let stand for 10 minutes.

3. Line a colander with a double layer of cheesecloth.

4. Strain the milk into the colander to collect the curds.

5. Let the curds drain for half an hour - just long enough for a quick swim, or to dig up some clams to steam.

6. Serve your cheese with some fresh bread and whatever you've been able to forage!

Early morning, Golden Bay

Drain the salty curds.

Don't drip it on your toes!

A handy driftwood log will do instead of a colander.

QUARK (FROMAGE BLANC)

This German soft cheese is so simple and versatile to have in the kitchen that it becomes a low fat favorite of most home cheesemakers. It makes lovely baked cheesecakes and pies or a rich topping for baked potatoes. Fromage Blanc and Fromage Frais are French versions that use a slightly less aromatic culture, but produce similar cheeses.

Time: 45 minutes to prepare, 10 hours to culture, 6 hours to drain. Yield: 1lb 4 oz (525 g) Quark.

....

1 quart (1 liter) Whole or skimmed cow milk
½ Culture Cupboard® Soft Cheese sachet
½ Culture Cupboard® Vegetarian Rennet sachet
¼ cup Non-chlorinated water*

Non-reactive pan
Non-reactive colander
Country Trading Co.® Dairy Thermometer
Country Trading Co.® Fermenting Flask or
Wide-mouth vacuum food flask
Country Trading Co.® Organic Cotton Cheesecloth

1. Sterilize all equipment - see page 12.

2. Heat the milk in a non-reactive pan to 73°F, 23°C.

3. Remove from the heat and stir in the soft cheese culture until well mixed.

4. Put a lid on the pan and set milk aside in a draft-free place to culture for 60 minutes.

5. Warm the fermenting flask and container by filling with boiling water for a couple of minutes. Check the temperature of the cultured milk mixture and reheat to 73°F, 23°C before pouring it into the container..

6. Mix the rennet into the water and gently stir it into the warmed milk stirring briefly to combine.

7. Put the container in the flask and let it culture for 10 hours or until set. It has set when the curd breaks cleanly when cut with a knife, or the curd has contracted slightly showing a ring of whey around the edge.

Boiling water for 15 minutes will remove chlorine present. Let water cool completely before adding rennet.

8. Slice the curd into 2 inch (5 cm) squares. Let it rest for 5 minutes then line the colander with sterilized cotton cheesecloth and pour in the curds.

9. Drain over a bowl for 6-8 hours in a cool place, 59°F, 15°C.

10. Scoop the drained curd into a clean glass jar or bowl, date, label, cover and store in the refrigerator. Eat within 7 days.

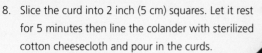

Tips for Using Quark

* Mix with herbs as a low fat topping for baked potatoes and wedges.

* Use as a perfect base for cheesecakes, quiches and pasta bakes.

* Make traditional German apple pie (A pfelkuchen).

* Drain for longer, mix with caraway seeds and serve with pretzels and beer.

* Mix with paprika, mustard, pickles, green herbs and spices for a homemade L iptauer cheese spread.

LABNEH (YOGURT CHEESE)

This soft yogurt cheese, also known as Labna, Lebbene and Labaneh across the Middle East, is quick to make and useful as a spread or rolled into savory cheese balls to serve with crackers.

Time: 10 minutes to make, 10 hours to drain. Yield: 1 quart (1 liter) yogurt yields 1-1 ½ cups (250-400 g) Labneh.

....

Plain yogurt
Chopped herbs, e.g. parsley, dill, mint, chives
Lemon juice
Salt and pepper
Ground cumin
A few drops of hot sauce

Non reactive colander
Country Trading Co.® Organic Cotton Cheesecloth

1. Sterilize all equipment - see page 12.

2. Line a colander with cheesecloth and place it over a large bowl.

3. Stir flavorings into the yogurt and pour into the colander.

4. For a soft, creamy cheese, let it drain for 10 hours in the refrigerator.

5. For a firmer cheese that you can roll into balls, fold the cheesecloth over the yogurt and place a clean plate on top with a weight. Press in the refrigerator for 10-15 hours depending on how firm you want the finished cheese.

6. When drained, store Labneh in a sealed container in the refrigerator and use within 7 days.

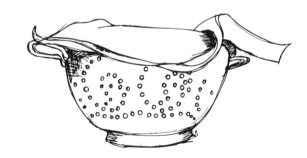

Make Labneh balls by gently rolling
teaspoonfuls of cheese between wet hands.
Place in a jar with enough olive oil to cover
them. This keeps them from drying out and
sticking together. Store in the refrigerator.

PANEER CHEESE

Paneer, or Panir, is a cooking cheese commonly used in Indian vegetarian dishes. It takes on the flavor of ingredients around it and because it is an unsalted cheese it can be used in both sweet and savory dishes. It also keeps its shape when cooked.

Time: 30 minutes to make, 3 hours to drain. Yield: 13 oz (370 g) Paneer.

2 quarts (2 liters) Whole cow milk
2 tablespoons Vinegar (wine or cider)

Non-reactive pans to make a double boiler
Non-reactive colander
Country Trading Co.® Dairy Thermometer
Country Trading Co.® Organic Cotton Cheesecloth

1. Sterilize all equipment - see page 12.

2. Gently heat the milk to 176°F, 80°C in a double boiler.

3. Add vinegar to milk while stirring. Mix gently for 15 seconds.

4. Continue heating to 194°F, 90°C and when the curds are well formed and the whey is a clear yellow color, line a colander with a double layer of cheesecloth and tip the curds and whey into the colander. Take care as the whey is very hot.

5. Gently push a little more whey out of the curds then tie the cheesecloth with string around the curds and hang it somewhere cool to drain for at least 3 hours.

6. Once drained, Paneer will be quite firm. Store in a container in the fridge for up to 7 days or freeze.

7. Cut into cubes for cooking.

TIPS:

Fry in butter and drizzle with honey for a nutritious dessert.

Marinate in tamari for use in vegetable stir-fry dishes.

Cube and cook in ghee with spices to add to vegetarian curries (see page 62 for Saag Aloo Paneer).

SERVING & MATCHING

Soft cheeses are food cheeses, made for cooking with and serving up with drinks and nibbles in a variety of dips and spreads. Here are some of our favorite accompaniments to serve with your homemade soft cheese creations, plus some ideas on what to wash them down with.

The light, lemony fresh flavors of soft cheeses like Quark, Cottage Cheese and Ricotta work well with light fruity wines, crisp lagers, hop beers and pilsners.

The rich and buttery flavors of Mascarpone, Cream Cheese and Sour Cream partner well with full-bodied aromatic wines and sparkling wines.

SOFT CHEESE PLATTERS

Are you tired of "cheese platter by numbers", with grapes, Blue, Brie and an aged Cheddar? Show some imagination and create platters with your soft cheeses that are all about taste and companion eating. Pair up soft cheeses with seasonal fruits, homemade crackers, fresh crunchy vegetables and toasted nuts to wow your tastebuds and your guests.

Herbed Labneh balls, knackebrod crackers & fresh cherries

Honey Ricotta, fresh strawberries & toasted almonds

Mascarpone & Blue Cheese with fennel sticks & brandy prunes

Soft Cheese Canapés

Soft cheeses are the friend of the drinks party menu. They form the base of numerous nibbles. Here are some of our favorites from savory to sweet. To be the host with the most, allow 6 per person, per hour.

Cream Cheese & smoked salmon on rye

Fresh radish with Cottage

Quark & leek baked tartlets

Mascarpone chocolate pot

Mascarpone & orange stuffed dates

Tomato, Crème Fraîche & avocado

Grape wrapped in Mascarpone and flaked almonds

Sweet potato cake with

Mini tiramisu with Mascarpone

Tamari marinated Paneer with sesame seeds

Quark & leek baked tartlets

Bruschetta with Ricotta, balsamic roasted beetroot & walnuts

Tomato, Crème Fraîche & avocado

...h & sour cream

Crowdie on oat cakes with orange marmalade

Rosemary & date mini scones filled with Crème Fraîche

TOASTED WALNUT & FIG SALAMI

If you have our Camembert book you will be familiar with this recipe. Apologies for including it here too, but it is just so perfect with cheese. If you are new to making fruit salamis, you will thank us for introducing you. They are combinations of chopped mixed nuts and dried fruit with just a little liquid to bind.

Time: 25 minutes. Yield: 1 lb (450 g), 45 servings.

Rolled into logs and wrapped, fruit salamis will last for 2 months in the refrigerator or they can be frozen. Sliced into little rounds, they make a wonderful addition to cheese platters. If you make them firm enough, they can even replace a cracker.

We have given you the recipe for our favorite combination, but please experiment with different dried fruits and nuts. If you come up with something sublime please let us know.

1 ½ cups Walnuts
1 cup Dried figs
1 cup Dried prunes
2 tablespoons Fruit paste or 1 tablespoon jam
2 tablespoons Orange juice
Zest of half an orange

1. Heat the oven to 300°F, 150°C and bake the walnuts on a shallow tray until they start to brown (5-10 minutes).

2. Finely chop the figs and prunes and mix together in a large bowl.

3. In a small saucepan, whisk together the fruit paste or jam and the orange juice on a low heat until combined.

4. Chop the walnuts into small chunks, so that they add a nice crunch to the salami, and mix well with the fruit using clean hands.

5. Add half the orange mixture to the fruit and nuts and combine well. Check the consistency and if it is not too tacky, add the remaining orange juice mixture.

6. Separate the mixture into 3 sausage-shaped pieces and place each piece on a square of plastic film.

7. Wrap the plastic film around the roll, leaving the ends open and roll each piece into a log. This keeps your hands and counter top clean. These are very rich, so small discs are more enjoyable (and economical).

8. Twist the ends of the plastic film closed and store the salamis in the refrigerator or freezer until required.

9. Slice into thin discs for serving and top with a dollop of soft cheese.

Tips:

Add port, rum or orange liqueur instead of juice for a festive twist.

Roll in cacao powder before slicing for a bitter chocolate coating.

If using homemade dried fruit, soak it in warm water or wine for 15 minutes, to soften.

ROY'S OAT CAKES

Behind every great topping is a good cracker. This oat cake is a refined cracker that makes a perfect austere partner for rich creamy soft cheeses and dips. We have tried many oat cake recipes but this one is the best.

Time: 20 minutes to make, 15 minutes to cook. Yield: About 50 small crackers.

It comes to us courtesy of New Zealand food writer Lois Daish, from her wonderful book "A Good Year". It is from her good friend Roy, and she gives the crackers a little extra roll with the rolling pin after they've been cut to make them super thin.

1 cup Wholegrain rolled oats
1 cup All-purpose flour
½ teaspoon Salt
¼ teaspoon Baking soda
½ stick (60 g) Butter
½ cup Boiling water

1. Heat the oven to 340°F, 170°C and line 2 oven trays with baking paper.
2. Process the oats in a food processor until they are broken down a little. Mix together with the remaining dry ingredients in a bowl.
3. Combine the butter and boiling water until the butter melts then pour into the dry ingredients.
4. Knead the mixture until it holds together.
5. Turn mixture out onto a lightly floured bench and knead it a little more, then roll it out very thinly.
6. Cut into small squares with a sharp knife and place the crackers on lined oven trays. Poke each cracker with a fork for extra flatness.
7. Cook for 10-15 minutes until light brown and crisp. Watch them closely as they will burn quickly.
8. Cool thoroughly on racks. Store in sealed glass jars for up to 1 month.

KNACKEBROD SWEDISH CRACKERS

This recipe is adapted from Wendyl Nissen of Green Goddess fame. It has become our favorite for serving with soft cheeses. The recipe makes a large quantity, which is great to have over the holiday season for entertaining and giving. A jar of these with some fresh Ricotta makes a lovely gift.

Time: 20 minutes to make, 2 hours to bake. Yield: 200 medium crackers or 3 x 1 quart (3 x 1 liter) jars.

....

8 oz (220 g) Wholemeal or white flour or a mixture
8 oz (220 g) Rolled oats (wholegrain recommended)
2 teaspoons Salt
5 ½ oz (155 g) Sunflower seeds
2 ½ oz (70 g) Sesame seeds
2 ½ oz (70 g) Linseeds
2 oz (60 g) Pumpkin seeds
1 ¼ pints (650 ml) Warm water
1 tablespoon Olive oil

1. Heat the oven to 265°F, 130°C. Line 4 oven trays with baking paper.

2. Combine all the dry ingredients in a large bowl then mix in the water and oil.

3. Let the mixture rest for 10 minutes. The mixture should be the consistency of wet porridge (it won't look very promising at this stage).

4. Spread a quarter of the mixture very thinly onto each tray, using a spatula. Don't be afraid to spread it to the point where you see the odd bit of baking paper; it does hold together when cooked.

5. Bake for 15 minutes then remove the trays from the oven and score the crackers into small squares using a pizza cutter or large, sharp knife.

6. Return trays to the oven and bake for up to a further 2 hours. Check after an hour – depending on your oven and how thickly you've spread the mixture, you may need the full 2 hours. Take them out when the crackers start to turn a nice golden color and are crisp.

7. Cool crackers completely then pack into jars with airtight lids. They will keep well for several weeks (not in our house!).

LAVOSH

These wafer-thin crispy slivers of cracker are like eating air with seeds and spices sprinkled on top. They are perfect with any thin sour cream dip or Labneh balls – nothing too heavy or your guests will be playing retrieve the lavosh.

Time: 30 minutes to make, 10 minutes to cook. Yield: 2 x ½ gallon (2 x 2 liter) jars, or 6 oven trays of crackers.

....

Crackers:
2½ cups All-purpose flour
1 teaspoon Granulated white sugar
1 teaspoon Salt
1 egg
½ cup (150 ml) Water
1 tablespoon Melted butter
Topping:
1 Egg, beaten with 2 tablespoons water
2 tablespoons Sesame seeds
1 tablespoon Poppy seeds
1 teaspoon Cumin seeds
1 teaspoon Sea salt

1. Combine flour, sugar and salt in a large bowl.

2. Mix the egg, water and melted butter together in a small bowl.

3. Add the wet ingredients to the dry ingredients and combine well until smooth.

4. Cover the dough and refrigerate for at least 30 minutes and up to an hour if you can.

5. Heat the oven to 375°F, 190°C. Line 5 oven trays with baking paper (you may need to bake in several batches if you don't have enough trays).

6. Cut the dough into 5 pieces and roll each one on a floured surface into a very thin sheet.

7. Put each piece of rolled dough on a lined baking tray. With a pastry brush, coat well with the beaten egg and water mixture. Be generous as it helps the seeds stick after cooking.

8. Mix the seeds and salt together and sprinkle over the top of the rolled dough from a reasonable height – not thickly, just a sprinkle. You can change the seed mixture to your taste; sometimes we put in caraway or chili flakes. The sesame and poppy seeds are a good base.

9. Take a heavy knife (light ones bunch and rip your dough) and score the sheet of dough into irregular shards. We like long pizza slice shapes – these crackers look best in uneven wedges, not nice little squares.

10. Put the trays in the oven and cook for 7-10 minutes. If you separate the trays well you can cook 2 trays at a time; if you cook the trays close together you don't get even browning of the crackers. Watch them like a hawk though, because one minute they're white and the next they are mahogany.

11. When the sheets are starting to brown and feel crisp, not doughy, take them out and cool them on a rack.

12. When completely cooled, break up the sheets into their pieces.

13. Store the crackers in a glass jar with an airtight lid. They will keep well for 2 weeks.

COOKING WITH SOFT CHEESES

When you make your own soft cheeses it is easy to have a couple on hand for use in your daily menu. Stocking your refrigerator with a creamy cheese and a lean cheese from our recipes will give you plenty of options for cooking up cheesy treats. Here are some of our favorite recipes for cooking with soft cheeses. We hope some of them become your favorites too.

SAVORY BAKED CHEESECAKE

When you need to turn out a pie, quiche, flan or cheesecake, Quark is the "go-to" cheese. This is an easy, tasty pie that we make all the time with whatever ingredients we have to hand. It is equally good with asparagus or red pepper and corn in the filling.

Time: 30 minutes to make, 20-30 minutes to cook. Yield: 1 x 11 inch (28 cm) round pie dish.

....

Wholemeal Pastry:
1 cup Wholemeal flour
1 oz (30 g) Butter, softened
1 teaspoon Tomato sauce (ketchup)
¼ teaspoon Salt
Up to ½ cup Milk or yogurt

Pie Filling:
1 cup Free-range bacon
1 medium Onion
Ground black pepper
Butter or ghee for frying
1 tablespoon Fresh parsley
5 Free-range eggs
½ teaspoon English mustard powder
10 oz (280 g) Quark
Optional toppings - grated cheese and bread crumbs

1. Heat the oven to 350°F, 180°C.

2. To make the pastry, combine the flour, butter, sauce and salt in a food processor and add milk until the mixture forms a ball and you have a stiff dough. Cover and refrigerate while you make the filling.

3. Grease an 11 inch (28 cm) round pie dish with butter. Roll out the pastry on a lightly floured surface and line the dish.

4. Chop the bacon and onion and fry in a little butter or ghee until lightly browned. Season with pepper and parsley.

5. Blend the eggs, mustard and Quark.

6. Add the bacon to the egg mixture and pour into the pastry case. Top with grated cheese and breadcrumbs (optional).

7. Bake for 20-30 minutes or until a skewer comes out clean and the filling has slightly risen.

8. Serve warm or cold with a green salad and potato salad.

SAAG ALOO PANEER

Paneer is a great cheese for absorbing whatever flavors you throw at it. This makes it a perfect base for a range of spicy curry dishes. One of our favorites is this spicy spinach curry also known as palak paneer. This makes an impressive vegetarian main dish and takes very little time to prepare with our one pan method.

Time: 30 minutes to cook with pre-prepared cheese. Yield: Serves 4 as a light meal with rice and naan bread.

....

2 tablespoons Ghee or butter

7 oz (200 g) Paneer

1 lb (500 g) Fresh mature spinach leaves

1 Onion

2 Cloves garlic

½ teaspoon Salt

1 teaspoon Ground ginger

1 teaspoon Garam masala

1 teaspoon Ground turmeric

¼ teaspoon Chili flakes

1. In a large heavy frying pan melt 1 tablespoon of the ghee or butter. Cut the Paneer into cubes and fry over a low heat until nicely browned on all sides. Set aside.

2. Wash and roughly chop the spinach and add it to the pan, sauteing it over a low heat until well wilted. Remove from the pan and squeeze any remaining moisture from the spinach so it is quite dry.

3. Add the remaining tablespoon of ghee or butter to the pan. Finely chop the onion and cook it on a low heat until it is clear but not browned.

4. Finely chop the garlic and add it to the onion to cook for a minute before stirring in the salt and remaining spices.

5. Cook the onion and spice mixture for 5 minutes on a low heat then add the cheese and stir together so the spices coat the cheese.

6. Finally add the spinach and stir it through to warm before serving.

7. Serve with flat breads, a bowl of rice and a yogurt dressing.

If you prefer a moist curry, don't
drain the spinach and stir in some
cream or chopped tomato in the final
2 minutes of cooking.

RICOTTA CANNOLI

Make authentic Sicilian cannoli with your own homemade Ricotta. Our cannoli tips include making the cases a few days ahead, adding a dash of liqueur to the filling and using a pasta machine to roll the dough to the right consistency. You will need some metal cannoli tubes to wrap the dough around while cooking.

Time: Cases 60 minutes, filling 20 minutes to make, several hours to chill. Yield: Makes 12 filled cannoli.

Cases:
1 cup All-purpose flour
¼ teaspoon Salt
¼ teaspoon Ground cinnamon
1 tablespoon Granulated white sugar
1 Free-range egg
1 oz (30 g) Butter
1/3 cup Port wine
Vegetable oil for frying

Filling:
1 lb (500 g) Ricotta
1 cup Confectioner's sugar
1 tablespoon Liqueur (Amaretto or Cointreau are nice)
¼ teaspoon Ground cinnamon
1 teaspoon Natural vanilla extract

1 teaspoon Fresh orange zest
1 teaspoon Fresh lemon zest
¼ cup Chocolate chips

1. To make the cases mix the flour, salt, cinnamon and sugar in a large bowl or mixer. Work in the beaten egg and chopped butter until well combined (save a little egg to seal cases).

2. Slowly add the wine until a stiff dough forms. Knead it until smooth then rest it for 30 minutes.

3. Cut the dough in half and roll out until very thin. If you have a pasta machine put it through No. 7 twice, then No. 5 and No.2.

4. Cut 4 inch (10 cm) circles from the dough and wrap them around the cannoli tubes, pressing the edges together with

a little egg so they don't come unstuck during cooking.

5. Heat vegetable oil in a wide deep pan (enough so that it will cover the cases) and when it is very hot cook the cases 2 or 3 at a time until golden. Remove and drain on kitchen paper towels. When cooled just long enough that you can handle the tubes, carefully twist the tubes to remove the cases. Store in a sealed container until use.

6. Mix all of the filling ingredients together in a large bowl until well combined and chill for several hours.

7. Just before serving, pipe the filling into the cases from each end with a piping tube and dust with a little more confectioner's sugar.

Try dipping one end of the cases in melted chocolate before filling or adding chopped pistachio nuts to the filling.

TIRAMISU

Once you start making your own Mascarpone you will want to explore the world of luscious desserts that you can make with this dreamy soft cheese. Tiramisu is a great place to start. This Italian favorite is always a show stopper and a great make ahead dish.
Time: 40 minutes to make, 4 hours to chill. Yield: Serves 8.

6 Free-range egg yolks

1 ¼ cups Granulated white sugar

1 ¼ cups Mascarpone

1 ¾ cups Whole cream (approx. 35% fat)

6 oz (170 g) Lady finger biscuits (Savoiardi)

3 tablespoons Marsala wine or a coffee liqueur

1 cup (250 ml) Espresso coffee

Extra whipped cream for topping

Cacao powder for dusting

Dark chocolate for garnishing

Fresh seasonal fruits

1. Gently whisk the egg yolks and sugar for 10 minutes in a double boiler over a low heat to thicken but not cook solid.

2. Remove from the heat and cool for 5 minutes then beat until thick.

3. Add the Mascarpone and blend well with a whisk.

4. Whip the cream until stiff peaks form. Lightly fold the whipped cream into the Mascarpone mixture.

5. Take the sponge biscuits and split them in half. Line the bottom of your bowl with some of the split biscuits.

6. Mix the wine or coffee liqueur and coffee. Brush the biscuits with some of the coffee liqueur mixture.

7. Layer the Mascarpone mixture, biscuits and coffee liqueur mixture until you use up all the biscuits.

8. Finish with a layer of the Mascarpone mixture, extra whipped cream, and dust the top with cacao powder and shaved chocolate. Garnish with fruit.

9. Refrigerate for at least 4 hours before serving.

CANNELLONI

Here is another cheese-fest of a recipe from Italy that cooks all over the world have adopted. High on the list of comfort cuisine, cannelloni is not a lean meal, but when you need hearty fare it is great. It also freezes and reheats very well.

Time: 40 minutes to make, 4 hours to chill. Yield: Serves 8.

....

20 Cannelloni pasta tubes

Filling:
1 teaspoon Butter
2 cloves Garlic
10 ½ oz (300 g) Fresh spinach
12 oz (340 g) Ricotta
2 oz (55 g) Parmesan
½ teaspoon Ground or grated nutmeg
1 tablespoon Fresh marjoram
Salt and pepper
2 Free-range eggs

Tomato Sauce:
2 cloves Garlic
1 small Onion
1 tablespoon Olive Oil
14 oz (400 g) can Tomatoes

¼ cup Red wine
1 cup Fresh basil leaves

Cheese Sauce:
2 oz (55 g) Butter
¼ teaspoon Ground or grated nutmeg
2 tablespoons All-purpose white flour
1 ½ cups Whole milk
4 oz (115 g) Cheddar cheese

1. Heat the oven to 350°F, 180°C and grease a large baking dish with olive oil.

2. To make the filling, place the butter and chopped garlic in a large frying pan and cook for 1 minute on a low heat.

3. Add the chopped, washed spinach and cook until wilted. Set aside in a bowl to cool.

4. Mix Ricotta, grated Parmesan, nutmeg, chopped marjoram and salt and pepper to taste. Then mix in beaten eggs.

5. Squeeze any moisture from the spinach and add to the Ricotta mixture.

6. To make the tomato sauce, fry the finely chopped onion and garlic in olive oil until translucent then add the tomatoes and red wine and reduce on a low heat for 10 minutes. Add the fresh basil and set aside.

7. To make the cheese sauce, melt the butter in a medium pan, add the nutmeg and flour and cook for 3 minutes. Whisk in the milk slowly until you get a nice thick sauce. Add the grated cheese, stir well and remove from the heat.

8. To assemble the cannelloni, stuff the pasta tubes with the filling and arrange in the greased baking dish.

9. Pour the tomato sauce over the cannelloni tubes and top with the cheese sauce.

10. Bake in the preheated oven for 25-30 minutes or until golden and allow to rest for 10 minutes before serving.

MORE SOFT CHEESE CUISINE

Of all the cheese families, soft cheeses are most at home in the kitchen. Here are some more ways we love to use homemade soft cheeses in our day-to-day cooking.

....

- Ricotta bakes very well to create a firm cheese that can be served warm with fresh herbs and a tomato salsa or left to cool and used as a grating or shaving cheese in salads.

- A couple of tablespoons of cream cheese, tossed through warm pasta with torn basil leaves and chopped ham, makes a delicious creamy dish.

- Mascarpone whipped with maple syrup makes a lovely dessert served with a bowl of fresh pitted sweet cherries or strawberries.

- Sour Cream mixed with chopped fresh herbs and a little smoked paprika makes an excellent dip or topping for baked potatoes.

- Make a lovely light salad with cottage cheese, finely chopped fennel bulb, grated apple, walnuts, cumin and lemon vinaigrette. Add a can of flaked drained tuna to turn it into a light meal.

- Cream cheese, cucumber and smoked salmon on rye makes for one classy sandwich.

- Dates stuffed with sweetened Mascarpone are a dainty snack with coffee when a full dessert is not required.

- Add a mixture of Quark and beaten eggs to drained cooked pasta with chopped herbs, vegetables and meat or smoked fish for a versatile pasta bake.

- Fold a spoonful of sour cream into hearty soups before serving for added richness and a pleasant acidity.

- Make a creamy mustard dressing for potato salad with wholegrain mustard and Fromage Blanc.

- Shavings of smoked Ricotta make a lovely topping for chicken and cranberry pizza.

- Cubed Paneer fried in ghee or butter and drizzled with runny honey makes a sweet snack.

- Cream cheese is the ultimate frosting for carrot cake, the secret to the perfect cheesecake and the best bagel spread.

- Sour cream makes a beautiful moist, gluten free, lemon and almond cake.

Ricotta Infornata, a baked Ricotta, is baked or dried in a warm oven to harden and preserve the cheese. It is excellent for shaving over salads and serving on cheese boards.

Tips & Troubleshooting

Making cheese at home is all about learning. There are a hundred and one things that can go wrong and often it is a combination of more than one of them causing you problems! But don't let that put you off. We've made most of the mistakes that you will make and we've improved our recipes and tips to try to help you avoid them.

One of the first mistakes we make is usually in our heads, not our kitchens. We have an idea of cheese - its taste and texture - based on what we buy at the deli and supermarket. Homemade cheese will be different and often much better, so keep an open mind while your senses get used to soft cheeses without additives.

DO I HAVE TO MEASURE pH?

I made great cheese for years without giving pH a second thought. Making cheese at home is not supposed to be a science project, right? Yes, but there comes a point where an understanding of acidification is really useful.

A pH of 7 is neutral. Below 7 is acidic and above is alkaline. The lower the number the more acidic it is. Fresh milk is slightly acidic with a pH of 6.5-6.8.

Acid levels are increased during cheesemaking by the action of starter cultures or acids such as lemon juice, vinegar or citric acid. This acidity helps the milk form good curds, expel whey, develop desired flavors and textures and preserve the cheese.

Time, quantity and temperature are the three main things that influence acidity in cheesemaking. For a given recipe you can over acidify by culturing for too long, adding too much culture or acid, or culturing too quickly on a high heat. Likewise you can under-acidify your milk by not culturing for long enough, using inactive culture or not keeping the milk warm enough during culturing to create the right acid level for that recipe.

Each cheese has its own optimum pH to be reached at each point in its creation. Some cheeses like Quark have a long culturing period at low temperatures to get them to their desired acidity, while others like Ricotta need a short time at a high temperature to achieve the right acidity. Wrong levels of acidity at each stage can lead to mushy, flabby curds and flavor, moisture and texture problems in the finished cheese. If your culture hasn't done its job and developed acid the cheese may be susceptible to spoilage bacteria that could form a health risk.

So do you need to measure it precisely? As long as you're following a good recipe, using good starters and good milk you don't need to measure pH.

But if you are interested in developing as a cheesemaker, get some pH strips or a meter and start taking readings. If you are having unexplained errors with your cheeses, ask if time, quantity or temperature might be contributing factors in getting the acidity levels wrong.

KEEP RECORDS

One of the best things you can do to improve your cheesemaking is to make notes in a cheesemaker's Journal so that when you have failures and successes you know what you did. Here's a picture of my journal. As you can see it isn't meticulous but then neither am I, so I understand it!

I've found the best way to get to your version of perfect for a given cheese is to keep making it and alter only one thing each time. You might try a different milk, culturing it for longer, adding more or less rennet, draining for longer, adding more or less salt. Good notes will help you work out what difference these changes make to your end cheese.

Keep a detailed journal

WHY IS MY CURD SOFT & FLABBY?

Sometimes your curd just doesn't firm up. It can happen in Quark, Sour Cream, Cottage Cheese and Cream Cheese. You get a mushy mess when you go to cut or stir it. Here are several things to investigate:

- Are you using good quality milk? Highly heat treated and homogenized milks can form weak curds. Try a different lightly pasteurized whole milk.

- Did you leave it long enough? Be patient. Many of the soft cheeses have a long, slow setting period. Don't be afraid to leave it a little longer if you put a knife into it and it isn't firm.

- Was it warm enough? In winter, milk can lose heat while culturing. Make sure you're keeping it at the temperature in the recipe, or between 68°F - 86°F (20°C - 30°C) if the recipe isn't specific.

- What strength of rennet do I have and am I using the right amount? Has it been stored in the refrigerator and is it still within its use-by date?

WHY IS MY CREAM CHEESE CRUMBLY?

The first reason is that it doesn't have any added gums and gels in it that give store bought cream cheese that sticky, tacky feeling in your mouth. But that doesn't mean your homemade cream cheese has to be crumbly. Here are some things you can do to get a moist and smooth cream cheese:

- Use homogenized milk! Yes it is the only cheese we recommend using homogenized milk for but it does lead to a creamier product.

- Don't be in a rush to cut the curd - let the acidity really develop into a good tangy curd before you cut it.

- Don't be tempted to add extra cream - you will get a creamier cheese by keeping the final fat content around 10-12%.

- Drain it in a cool place like the refrigerator and whip the salt into it halfway through draining as per the recipe on pg. 22.

- Don't press it as this will dry the curd too much.

NOT A LOT A RICOTTA?

Skimming Ricotta into molds should be like fishing for clouds. You should be scooping up light and fluffy bundles of air-filled curds to put into your molds for draining and the remaining whey should be a pale, clean and clear straw yellow color. If your Ricotta making is more like grasping at wisps of wind, here are some tips:

- Don't over-stir after you've added the acid - just give it a brief mix and let it sit.

- Be patient - let it rest for the time prescribed without poking it too much. Just gently draw curds away from the sides every now and then. Don't stir it. Let the clouds form.

- If you are making traditional whey Ricotta then your yield will be lower than with milk. Make sure your whey is fresh and not overly acidic to start with.

- Don't add too much acid - this can make fine, grainy, hard curds that sink like a stone, not float like a cloud. If in doubt add the acid in two portions.

- Do concentrate on the temperatures for adding the salt and the acid. Don't overheat it.

- Don't be in a hurry to scoop out the curds. If you haven't over-acidified it, the curds will form a happy clump on top of your pot, gathering in more protein from the whey while they wait. Stirring is the enemy of fluffy Ricotta.

WHY IS MY CHEESE BITTER?

We are aiming for a sweet lactic tang in our homemade cheeses. We should be able to taste the milk, sometimes a little salt and in cultured cheeses a pleasant, clean cheese flavor. If you're getting bitter notes in soft cheeses here are the three usual suspects:

- Too much rennet - use only as much as required to set the curds.
- Culturing for too long leads to over acidification of the curds.
- Not enough salt to balance the flavors and assist with the drainage.

THE SECRET TO CREAMY SAUCES?

Now you are making your own soft cheeses you will want to get saucy! Here are some good tips for making creamy sauces without ending up in a big curdley mess!

- The richer the soft cheese the better it will be for creamy sauces - sauce loves fat!
- Always add your soft cheese to your sauce or dish just before serving to avoid curdling while it sits around.
- Keep the temperature of your dish well below boiling when you add the soft cheese. Heat will curdle your cheese quicker than you can say mac'n'cheese! 160°F, 70°C is safe.
- Acidic ingredients will also curdle your creamy cheeses, so only add them to dishes without a lot of vinegar, lemon juice or wine. A little bit of wine is okay in a sauce if is well cooked out before you add your creamy cheese.
- If your creamy sauce does split, cool it rapidly by putting the pot in a sink of cold water and whisking it, adding a little more soft cheese to bring it back together.

IMPROVISING CHEESE MOLDS

As modern home cheesemakers, you can get any number of plastic molds and hoops to help you drain and shape your cheese - but you can also use what you have to hand just as effectively. The reality is that most of the soft cheese in the world is made in kitchens with basic improvised equipment that does the job just fine.

We have even been known to use a box of snow chains to press our cheese! The key to success with all of these improvised molds is making sure anything that comes in contact with the cheese is sterilized and non-reactive. If the weather is warm, place the molds in the refrigerator while draining. Here are some of our favorite improvised cheese molds.

Make a firmer cheese by wrapping curds in cheesecloth and pressing between sterilized chopping boards or serving platters. Sterilized rocks, gym weights or cans of beans can all work as weights!

Tomato paste tins make cute little soft cheeses for use on cheese boards or desserts (make sure they have a coated non-reactive lining).

Your kitchen colander lined with sterilized cotton cheesecloth is a very effective mold for draining Quark, Fromage Blanc or Sour Cream.

You can also tie the cloth with string and hang it to let gravity press the curds.

Traditionally Italian Ricotta was drained through round baskets made from reeds. The light, finely woven wicker baskets used to serve bread, fries and sides in restaurants make perfectly fine Ricotta molds if you sterilize them well.

BEHIND THE SCENES

I don't know who had the idea to photograph these books in our little house, but it has been great. The end result is a real slice of Country Trading Co.®

Daniel Allen, the man behind the camera, balances on kitchen stools while we ask for everything, from every angle. He is a joy to work with and he likes cheese!

Geraldine styled the shots, did the post-processing and illustrations, was chief hand and apron model and cannelloni maker!

Geraldine & Dan sample Ali's canapés.

Drying cheesecloth & mats in the porch.

On this book our friends Ali and Canada also came in to lend a hand. Ali worked her magic on the canapés for the spread on page 50, after which we sat on the porch and ate them all.

Canada came in bearing Tiramisu, Cannoli, Savory Cheesecake and a bottle of whisky. We ate the Tiramisu and Cannoli, but her husband wanted the whisky back. She also wrangled cheeses and props for several other lovely shots. Both ladies gave the little kitchen quite a workout!

Heather

Ali with a brace of her beautiful canapés.

Say Cheese Canada!

OTHER TITLES...

Now you've mastered soft cheese, explore the other titles in our home dairy "how to" range.